Ugh Ugh Ocean

Ugh Ugh Ocean

Joanna Fuhrman

Hanging Loose Press
Brooklyn, New York

www.hangingloosepress.com

Printed in the United States of America
10 9 8 7 6 5 4 3 2 1

Hanging Loose Press thanks the Literature Program of the New York State Council on the Arts for a grant in support of the publication of this book.

Cover painting by Nina Bovasso, *With You in Mind* #2 (detail), from the collection of Agnes Scott College, Decatur, Georgia

Cover design by Pamela Flint

Grateful acknowledgment to the publications where some of these poems first appeared: *6 x 6*, *Brooklyn Rail*, *Seattle Research Project: Experimental Theology*, *Fort Necessity*, *Hanging Loose*, *Lit*, *New American Writing*, puppyflowers.com, *Sad Little Breathings & Other Acts of Ventiloquism*, *Saint Ann's Review* and *Xconnect*.

I want to send special thanks to Jean-Paul Pecqueur, Aaron Kunin, David Hess, and Noelle Kocot whose thoughtful comments I always value. Additional thanks to David Shapiro for inspiration and encouragement, to the Clemente Gallery, Nina Bovasso and Agnes Scott College for letting HL reproduce part of the painting, to the editors Dick, Bob, Ron, Mark and Marie. And to everyone associated with The Poetry Project for making me feel at home. Also, of course, to my parents.—JF

Library of Congress Cataloging-in-Publication Data
Fuhrman, Joanna
  Ugh ugh ocean / Joanna Fuhrman.
    p. cm
  ISBN 1-931236-17-8 (pbk.) -- ISBN 1-931236-18-6 (cloth)
    I. Title.

PS3556.U3247 U38 2003
811'.54--dc21

2002038776

Produced at The Print Center, Inc. 225 Varick St., New York, NY 10014, a non-profit facility for literary and arts-related publications. (212) 206-8465

Contents

Prayers for Business

"A man in the sea is waving and screaming "Help"
And the echo is replying, "What do you mean by that?"
—Jules Supervieille
(translated by George Bogin)

MEANS OF ENTRY

A Quiet Poem

Your water is still when it gushes & I envy this
said Zeus to the fire hydrant. Compared to you
my strength is clumsy: the color red in a pastel field.
I have spent too many evenings ripping
stars out of the dark's Laundromat.

I am sorry for your sadness, said
the hydrant to Zeus, but I can't unleash
the quiet you desire. There is a need
for the highway to tremble
with televised cruelty.

Just because you long to see the sunset
reflected in the public swimming pool,
doesn't mean children aren't crashing waves
there, happy with the quiet they destroy.

So Zeus left and the world
continued as it always pretended to,
the god eating baked beans
with his servant in the cloud palace,
the hydrant watching the trees
record their own destiny,
the children dragging their older siblings
by the ear through the main section
of town and calling it love.

Means of Entry

Window

A dead or sleeping bird dangles
from a tree. I can read my fortune based
on the direction it hangs: north for love,
east for money. The milkmaiding of the harp
softens the blow to deem it no knock at all.
Hear me Hear me I whisper into my pillow.
I just wanted to promise someone something
or other—not the excess of the post-Nixon-era brain,
but a nice little square: a quasi-oceanic flesh module.

Door :

We take showers in different apartments
while it rains outside. The unbridled riddle
of eagle season gives our cells a new lease.
If you were here, you'd laugh at me
for trying to siphon the last drop of beauty
from space, as if I could create a new
idea of space, separate from our need
to live in it and think we know it.
The top of a radish rots in a puddle.
Nothing is ever *just* sad.

Orpheus' Post-Orphic Confessions

The sun was a dying fish in the sky
so I took the job as adman. Can you blame me?
You try eking a living singing about
chop suey addicts and balloon animal
connoisseurs. Yeah, I begged
the moon for help, but truth is,
I prefer her as a casual appliance.

It isn't that I'm against the soul or anything:
it's one of my embarrassing favorites
like that light blue blanket with my childhood drool
dried on it. Sometimes, when I dream about
you-know-who, I carry a piece of it with me,
secret, folded in my pocket, snuggled
against my mini-dictionary of Portuguese curses
and the cat hair from the temporary lover's abode.

The poems, never really mine,
continue to write themselves—
in the rows of spinning dryers on 13th Street,
in the saliva of a sleeping stranger,
in the space between milk and a toasted O,

so now as fall breaks into its delectable rash,
enacting its critique of pure ego and such,
I no longer bark in competition
with the toothy stars or their invisible
high-falutin' motion.

I like life now. I've grown fond
of sharpening pencils in the closet with my teeth.
I can eat a peach without comparing
it to birth. Even the cat's fine;
the woman with the birthmark on her thigh
looks enough like Eurye in the dark,
to keep him from wailing.

Life Trajectories (The Capsule Version)

Ex-Celebrity

Once that woman was a famous rat trainer.
Now, even the jukebox rejects her quarters.

Smart Guy

He's coded the ocean's apparent chaos,
found himself in the cyber-waves. Still,
the swirling of a crowded party confounds him;
he'll never navigate his way to the wine.

Sandpiper

Open the brown bag of a night sky and find
another sky, doubled over like a sick child.
This is the place where nothing hurts—
the flicker of a light bulb on a bright day.

Twins

At three, they share a lion's costume.
When they are dead even their mother
won't know which son is which.

Post-Feminist

Am I just another car alarm, wailing at the moon?
thought the car alarm, wailing at the moon.
The circles of boys who knew where on the ear
to blow are now just a single butterfly,
swept like a wildfire's last ash
into the outline of a once house.

Failed Painter

Paul Klee said the artist should know his palate
instead of the world. One out of three dumb alter egos

might agree. #4 goes skinny-dipping in the exuberant
verbal culture of his fantasy wife. #2098,
the future love of his life, sews.

Grain of Sand

.

Superstar

In the space between a Milky Way candy bar
and the span of our galaxy, a superstar is born,
pretends to enjoy foie gras,
dies.

To the Tune of "Flight of the Slight Breeze"

Light on a candle flickers.

I feel nothing for you and then everything

and then nothing.

A fly in darkness draws

a silent line in space.

The same fly under fluorescent lights

once cleared children from a spill.

Stare at any word long enough—

its meaning leaves.

Rhapsodic Milkshake

1)

The ancient babysitter who started with the goal
of knitting her two-pound dog

a sweater finds herself too lonely
to ever admit it's done. "I just want

to be as barren as the seashell's nakedness
on the white Formica table,"

I explain to her through an olive green coffeemaker.

"Why do poets always feel the need
to talk through appliances?"

she asks in reply. Furry arm branches inside
fly every which way, perceptible

only to us and to the pet lizard.

2)

The ancient babysitter who started with the goal of swimming
across the Atlantic has had difficulty finding a suit. What thousand-
year-old self-respecting lady would enter the body of her possible
death adorned with hot pink stars?

3)

Still, I feel no pity for her or for anyone.

4)

Near an ocean crowded with swimming dogs,
an ancient babysitter struggles with a crossword.

Gray seagulls drop the bones of some family's fried chicken.

Near an ocean swimming with post-Socratic fleas,
ancient babysitters have been known to write poems

in donated cow's blood on driftwood.

What does it mean to be *known*?

The sun is as large as the sun in a movie.
The sun is as pale as the sticker of a sun on a fingernail.

Ancient babysitters have been known
to chip nails on barnacles.

Yeah. I envy them this.

On Glimpsing John Berryman Reborn as a Hasid

He's happier now. With G-D on his side.
The whole dad complex done; that in-
surmountable *why* dissolved like a tablet
in a tumbler of celery tonic. The suit
suits him fine, tricks him to feel he's
joined to some others, that he's not

just the sum of his words: a dog's
drooling tongue in an advert for what
was her name? He doesn't
need fame—that coat—
it never kept him warm.
Threadbare. All there.

It's much nicer, this life. No pressure
to trope his inner Jewness & women,
those divine torture devices,
no longer whisper from the margins
of his ripped poems, censoring
his mom's blunt warnings to behave.

To the Tune of "Multiplication Afternoon"

for David Shapiro

"At the end of the greatest volume of poetry all you have is a book in your hands"
—David Shapiro

I had already ripped out the page when its copy fell from the sky
and onto my newly quaffed peak and into a glass of soluble eyelids.
This was a time of my life when I was a big believer in disquisition,
or was it disquietude? Each night under the subset "headlining act,"
I would open a beer can with my teeth and a poetry book with my hands
and then, suddenly, there would be me, forged through a diffident avoiding.

There was, of course, a freedom to this. Imagine, if you will,
a redheaded ten-year-old in scuba gear and neck brace, multiplying
twelve-fingered digits by zero. She'd keep at it, until the absence
was so huge, all of us could cradle up inside, and then earth,
it would be the original flashing cursor of an eye sped up,
and me, I'd be a drop of cola on a lip, a flicked speck.

And So We Were Ricocheting

for Edmund Berrigan

Despite the unctuous rising of the mercantile tide, my guardian
rubber ducky fears nicht. We doorknob together as pals, lurching
from swell de jour to soup of the year. They say that merely know-
ing another mind, whether toy or human, is often enough to free
one from the pinnacles of a so-called "bow-wow youth." A new
unheard-of quiet can then infiltrate the fray. A sea anemone in a
bathtub, for example, or a paintbrush dressed up like a femme
fatale dressed up like Needles, California. I wonder who will help
me to divine the differences between all these blessed and furry
wags. The dry crown of the koan-spouting wig detests all of my
missed and glorious stabs.

Some Meditations on the Female Soul

for Adeena Karasick

Alone with the famous poets' pet rats
in the brassiere library, I attempt
to figure out the *human*,
to enforce a vulnerable blinking.

I might as well be a celebrity,
wearing stereoscopic glasses
for all I imagine and claim to understand.

I confess—I'm a stranger even
to the sandwich entering
my own mouth. Books piled high
like bodies just prove who's
written more, but still,

when I whisper that some mirrors
are more intimate with me
than my own shadow—

I mean this mirror
in particular, folded over
in its scalloped case,
reflecting its own
inaudible dark.

Knowledge Blobs

for Aaron Kunin

"Isn't it funny,/There's a Pacific Ocean,/ But no self?"
—Bob Perelman

1)

These doubts are like holding
a hand over a burning candle
to feel if it's hot.

As if it would be cold?

This is why it is said

a tugboat is needed—

to prove the existence of waves.

2)

I decided to mark my shoes. "Happy" on the left foot, "Sad" on the right. This way I'll know the difference. This way on days when the pencil sharpener decides to expire, the moon will no longer need to excuse itself from its role as courtship advisor. Space will replace the sky's blunt period with an equally predictable punch. As if to redefine habit as something inspiring passion in a burgeoning commissioner.

To be sure, one of us could have been a good girl. Dressed in a habit like a TV nun advertising the succulent error of prosperity. Yes, what we call music will always be a treat to dormant violins, but no more than any other packaged product questioning the petulance of breath.

Enough already with hairstyles, soccer cleats, toads!

Those objects that create the limits of desire limit the created desire of limit.

3)

Board a voice.

Calculate.

"Just throw a glass of water in my face and I'm happy."

Free as a dash in a crumpled letter—

Make me the last straight line.

My belief?

Trees.

Stable Self Blues

"It is odd to have a separate mouth."

—Bill Berkson

I'm just another pizza delivery girl
Without a pizza, a raconteur with nothing
To recount. I heavy-breathe by the rabbit
Iconography, refusing to multiply. Mina Loy
Is my favorite video game.
I love blowing up those enemy nouns.

Do you think we could escape into a city without nouns?
Be the thought-repressor gesture demanded of each girl
Who sticks her tongue into the game
Of another's ribs. With lights off, nothing
Could stun us more than a Mina Loy
Christmas tree, decorated with pink rabbit

Feet key chains. Oh no. Rabbits!
They're like a new breed of nouns
Multiplying like a couple of Mina Loys
Into a pointillist ex-girl
Paradise of verbs. Nothing
Could really be better than this game

In which nothing feels like it is a game,
And dead friendships like sick rabbits
Swirl a sonata into the single nothing
In the disarray of things. Damn nouns,
Please stop muting my explosions. You're too girly
Dressed to kill like Mina Loy,

Pretending you're just a minor Mina Loy.
Don't think I'm putting down all games.
I love the exquisite popcorn fiasco of those girls
Dancing until they turn into a thousand rabbits
Chewing on a slew of predigested nouns,
Swallowing the last of all those so-called "things."

I wish I could be happy to be just a thing,
To decorate the foyer like a post-poem Mina Loy,
To be content with all the useless nouns
Before they fracture into neon games.
Imagine what peace those rabbits
Could inspire if they stopped chewing the ribbons of the girls.

Who said nouns? I've enjoyed the migrating waves of game.
There's nothing really left to my memory of Mina Loy.
The stuffed rabbits on the pillow sleep like the sweetest smallest girl.

Retronormativity

The 1950s end for you in Eden
and end again under impressive tits.
This is a favorite clichéd history of reading,

and is, as well, the failure of our every meeting—
why I feel like such shit
when you claim the 1950s end for me in Eden.

Is this where all those words were leading?
You burn a match you claimed was never lit.
This is a favorite clichéd history of reading:

"a couple so in touch they don't need meaning."
I want to whittle down these words until they split.
The 1950s end for some in Eden.

Enough! To hell with all your dreaming!
It's as if you did not know that I could exit
your favorite clichéd history of reading.

I'm sorry if you find this all misleading.
Words spark beyond their surface blitz.
The 1950s end for you in Eden.
This is a favorite clichéd history of reading.

Near a Gregarious Passage # 8

Boulder in Sunlight

an inner tongue forages
for pardoned seals, becoming
hind or lulled hill-
minded hood summoning
another haunted "or"
before fangs groom
the of of (the?)

Boulder in Shadow

skin lunges out of flecked
passing. fails. tangled "ands"
threaded knobs. heed to it and
in. minus sorrow. folded over.
bulging. faced from. toothy.
billow. newborn. knob.

Boulder in the Dark

sucker-punched from logic
my. two-time-dig-a-link
~~screams~~. knees. please.
loose rabies. teeth. soldiers.
frisky scalawags. scheming.
fail me. one minus one.
smart-clocked. dart.

Admonitions

For Leslie

Despite the poisonous health food
Flying across the sunset or the rail track
Flooded with imagination
Rainwater, BAD STUFF
STILL HAPPENS
EVERYWHERE. You are like
The bouncing carrot
From the beyond.
The anorexic stewardess
Is just pretending
To be an Angel
Of Happiness. Bop her
On the head, dear.
Say "Bad stuff, bad."
Say "We are going
Everywhere at once
At the speed of a dark
Question mark and
Grammar will not help."

For Austin

The firetrucks remain, but you have already
Forgotten how I think.
Damn. I want my complexity
Back. Those are fingers
You place on your
Temples
To think. Leave them there
Will you?
I want to see if they are there
When I return.

For Katie

Thumb on the bullshit meter.
Can't I be self-indulgent for exactly two
Minutes and thirty-five seconds? You're so lucky
You can bend your back and flirt with boys
You'd never want to sleep with.
Don't worry if the famous poet doesn't
Remember that you played her door
In San Francisco. All that opening in a closed
World makes a smart chick dizzy. If you want,
Try opening a fragrant orange when there's no one
To smell it except the tree doctor,
Cutting down the forest. Katie,
It's winter already.
You've written some poems.
Stop thinking cold thoughts!

For Aaron

You make me want to be bored.
Will you bore me more with your talk
About being boring? If everything boring
Were like being bored by your boringness,
Then I'd hope that interestingness
Would vanish from the planet like the billions
Of brands of soda that might have existed
Had Coca-Cola not dominated the market
And replaced them all with loud anti-
Boring slogans, selling an idea of itself
To conceal the taste of the drink.
(Is that what ads do?) David Antin says
"Poetry is a commercial that sells nothing."
What am I trying to hide?

Dear Ms. Fuhrman,

It has come to our attention that you have been perpetuating a mistaken notion about the nature of cola advertising. The purpose of a slogan is not to hide the taste of a drink but to enlarge it. The words are part of a larger matrix, adding simultaneous pleasure to what you might naïvely call "authentic pleasure." Yes, some may infer that we are attempting to sell ideas of happiness, swimming pools, clean patriotic sex etc. as a substitute for the product in the can. But you should understand, all we offer is rooted in the flavor of the drink. The taste is the back of the turtle that the rest of the world, as they say in ancient Native American myth, is built on.

Sincerely,

R.T. Rulington
Director of Marketing, The Coca-Cola Corporation

For Noelle

Is a slotted spoon an orifice?
Why so many Orphic
Paper-cuts? Sing your new mind-
Old mind ditty. Yeah yeah.
You'll never write another
Poem except for the next one
You write. Until then,
You're at every meeting.
I'm at every reading. We will be
Banded together one day
In a celestial motel with love
For certain small lies and, yes, squid?

For Chris

You wear your "ifs" and "thens"
Like dangling earrings over Lake Erie.
Now in an actual present,
Matter detaches from time
And hangs over the water
Miriam has boiled for a bath.
Listen to those petals as they fall—

That's a lilac, not just a flower.
That's a poem you just wrote,
Not just a simulacrum of cultural capital.
It may never be early enough
In the next century to forgive
The sun its bifurcated display,
But forget it for a second.
Try gliding into the future
Without performing
A cost analysis on the past.

For Jean-Paul

No one reads philosophy anymore—
That monopattern of thinking
About thinking just spurs the epistemologist
To croon. The birds on all the rocks
Are the only beasts that long to read.
Listen to their country gossip:
That pre-Cartesian chirp
Abounds from every non-word
We thought one couldn't think.
J.P. It's here. Here.
In every not yet sentient leaf,
In every unthought thing.

Dear Joanna,

The words like pigeons scattered away from a running child keep
running away from you. You are too much a girl and too much not
a girl. Why so little lust here—such fake skepticism about the
weight of bodies and their natural trajectory?

I've heard you lying to other poets at the backs of bars, bullshitting
that your poems are gifts—that they create an alternative economy
in some sort of Utopian post faux-Marxist sense, but really, they
are just ways to convince yourself other people exist.

Love,

Jack

For Joanna

Drink chocolate milk.
Wear a yellow raincoat.
Tell everyone everything
About the depth of nothing and then
Quiz 'em on it.
Fail anyone
Who answers anything
Correctly.
Buy yourself a puppy.
Name it Failure.
Call out
  "Here, Failure, here."
Have sex with any stranger
Who thinks it's possible
You aren't calling him.

For Adeena (postscript)

Your daughter is flying
On two airplanes
At once. As a Jew you know
To carry luggage to look
Like a Jew. Duck already,
And help me duck,
From that off-duty
Ambulance. From its wide
White eyes,
From its quiet.
Adeena,
Throw out your suitcase!
Hoard all the suitcases of
The world and the anti-world
In your original suitcase.
Throw your passport
To what they say
Is the wind. Don't worry,
It's only a doll-sized fan.

INTERIORS

Letter from New York

Black buckets of frogs absorb
the last of evening's light.
In Rattray's last poem, he writes
the Greek root of calm is "bright."
As I write, I can hear the whir
of a neighbor's air conditioner.
A child practices flossing as she walks.
Sun eradicates the memory of rain.
I'm worrying, again, that the woman
in your dream who threatens to write
your portrait but doesn't think to look
at you is supposed to be me. Whenever
my cat gets his claws stuck in my clothes,
I have to undress. My student said *Prufrock's*
a love song, the way a bird calling
for an unknown mate sings a love song.
The Jewish star I got for Christmas shifts
in wind. All objective correlatives
are beautiful because they're false.
"Those birds, they're just warning
others off their property." In your dream,
the portrait (yours or mine?) turns into
a nation-sized tornado, then into a seed
too small to see. Its change reminds me
of the first set of tablets, the ones Moses
hauled from Mount Sinai, written on the purest
emerald ever seen: its secrets lost
once dropped. Still, my friend, for her kid's
Oz party, she claimed to know what
she was reviving when she poured
green Jell-O into the Emerald City mold.

Late May Serenade

A large silver button from my sweater is in my hand.
 "All language may as well be a way of hiding. "
If so, a painting of a single flower is only a symbol
of a woman once all real flowers have died
(which they have.) Wall, I want to pull *all*
the poetry books from your shelf to know
you still exist behind them. Anything
to keep me from spilling orange juice on the
carpeted floor. What more is there to the lush un-
speakable lucidity that allows caterpillars to crawl?
A boy I don't know tosses his hair; and a new
"rising dampness," reminds me (for a change?), not
of "an enraptured jungle blooming in Abyssinian dusk"
or of the old anthology's "glimmering legion
of Chinese nightingales," but of a fraying sock,
the left one, my lately naked toe.

Evidence

for Jessica Kagle

"It is less significant that you are a park ranger, than that you are in love."
—Jenny Smith

If you were not a park ranger, I would not
have met you. If I were not a park ranger,
you would not have met me. Neither of us
would be park rangers, so we would be strangers.

If we did *eventually* meet, neither of us park rangers,
we would have to scrounge around for non-park ranger
subjects to talk about; perhaps our families and their
bourgeoisie yards; how we hate those god-damned trellises,

or how awful the smell of perfume is when it cloaks
the burnt tofu scent of the garden grill. We could not
complain about our crazy boss or share the joy
of guiding the beer-drinking ruffians to the ugliest nook.

We would have to count the blue spotted salamanders
all alone, off hours, reading poetry books instead
of government guides, in our tourist T-shirts
with the park's name blazoned in peeling iron-on glitter.

Luckily though, we are both still park rangers!
May we forever wear these stiff brown
matching uniforms! May we always rise early
to unveil and polish our badges!

Interiors

In what I think of as your inner ocean,
waves crash backward, away from shore.

A beachcombing off-duty air traffic
controller visualizes a missing plane.

Even the lone seagull here is too kind to eat
the fish it suddenly realizes is in its own mouth.

Is it a violation of you for me to write like this,
as if I had access to your psyche's life?

They'll probably send me to poet-jail
or, God forbid, poet-hell where I'll have

to reread ad nauseam the lines I wrote
to other men before they broke my heart.

I hope you visit.

Until then it comforts me to write
as if I know you well. To pretend this poem

is a sort of lyric submarine, powered by the swishing
of optimistic pink goldfish and babbling clams.

In the Basement of the Museum of Potential Urges

Those greenish lights reveal the restroom's layered scum.
The faucet by the window is always on.
No water needed.

You might want to linger with your eighth-grade crush,
that vegetarian you inhaled veal near
in the prep school cafeteria. Her teeth are still so vertical.

Who cares if there are more "exciting" exhibitions
on the floors above: a rumor of some porno
projected on a fifth grade teacher's smile,
a stick of butter churned to never melt?

Desire here is so hush-hush that docents bow
their heads in admiration. I bet you never
knew that girl whose hair you tried to stroke
was still recovering from chemo?

And yes, it's true,
the gift shop's nearly out of souvenirs:
their buyer's too ashamed to check the inventory ...

but still, I want to meet you here.

Please bring the look you hid from me
when you turned fifteen. I'll shine
my nipples like the drool-wet stars.

Niagara

Silly me, why can't I embrace the dumb
mixed metaphors of this drunken night?

The angel's water-slide is still not dry.
The tadpoles are so horrified by the fig leaves
over their reflection they are forced to speak:

In their best Pavlovian dialect they whisper
"All I really wanted from the frog king
was a return to the glistening planet of the womb!"

But meaning, it's still here: shoving
its paws into a sutured hole,
shouting "divide my friend, divide."

So what? The stirring of a spoon
is nothing like my mind contracting, nor
is my hair like the active bats that spin
the book cave of your ears.

It is time to let loose the wild streetcars
and their streamers of light: the caterpillar toothache
of the stars explodes towards Tulsa.

Soon I will be required to Judy Garland
across a wide river. It may be too late then
to Will Rogers the void.

Fable

Even a wolf in my ex-lover's sweater
is more dangerous and beautiful if I love him.

This isn't a warning.

There's too much thought in my thinking
to dissolve into the spiraling trees.

The forest, let alone the jungle,
won't have it.

They say: cut open the intestine to feel intense.

They say: you've always been lousy with toys.

They don't care if breath is.

It's just so much harder than I thought,

being a person.

I keep wanting to roar a little,
to convince those invisible tigers that I'm with them,

wherever they are.

Bionic Vacation

Soon the robot union will demand
a loyalty oath. I will have to sign my name
onto your metal casing and you will
pretend it feels good. In the meantime,
there's a sandwich pile balanced high
on the head of a thumbtack: a ladybug
with only one spot saunters across a crumb.
Does it matter that we are said to be hollow,
that inside the paper bag where we meant
to put our lunch, souls of birds flap about?

My lips have never touched anyone's except
yours when you thought I was an empty soda bottle,
but that doesn't mean I don't root
for the camera woman each week to sweep
her crush into the narrow produce aisle
where the special effects guy has glued
all the stacked apples together,
as if this would help them not fall.

Ceremony

After the slaughter and our initial joy,
they roll out the TV cart with the giant's heart.
It is smaller than anyone had expected,
about the size of a cow's brain and almost

as dark. The effect of this is the opposite
of its claimed purpose. What's left of the giant

who had once cast a shadow
over the entire town is now
as small as the head of a nursing baby.

I miss our shared fear,
the feeling before sleep that we would
all perish by the same green hand.

All I can hear now is my younger sister
trying not to breathe because she fears
she will gasp too hard.

Holding the cold ventricles in my palm,
I know my memories were never mine.
That wasn't ever my thigh his finger

stroked the night his parents threw
the dishes down the stairs; even my tongue

which at one time seemed like
a horizon in the falling sky

sleeps now in some waking stranger's
mouth, numb.

Two Dogs

They sniff each other: each wet nose
carefully examining the other's wound

as a crowd devours the air around it.
I have noticed these dogs before.

One I pointed out to you last summer as it slept
under an elevated train. The other we both heard,

when it howled outside your window the first
night you wouldn't hold me. I wonder,

is this poem an apology for absent-minded dogs
everywhere or maybe it's some mutation

of a love poem I'm no longer
qualified to write. Either way,

the dogs will never tire of each other.
The cold nose on the wound

of the second dog will always remind it
that it was but is no longer bleeding.

Either way, the quiet they create
is almost large enough to swallow

our entire world, is large enough
to create a new world, a substitute

indistinguishable from this one
to everyone but them.

Meaningville

You made me want to Ping-Pong
through the leaf-filled living room, light
on my fingertips and tongue ends.

It was that old poem-as-visor routine:
seeing you and me where margins extend

past words and into the splints
of ourselves that ignite
and vanish in words.

It's true.

I know it's too late now to try
whittling sunrise to fit between
the lines of a lit parking lot.
We can never refill that particular
empty pickle barrel.

Still, what we think of as forest has yet
to be swallowed by the empty hive.

Those famous bees in sunglasses—
they're just waiting for someone
to ask them who they are.

Needhatch

1)

Just when I thought I'd escaped,
you arrive in your raincoat
and I'm supposed to imitate the rain?

Sorry sorry sorry sorry
says the wet headache.

Twelve years in a quenched
valley of cut asphalt and now this.

2)

We swam as if my strokes
were Japanese calligraphy.

Yours were Hebrew and thus unreadable

to me, or so they seemed, though I'm supposed
to be the "biological Jew."

We had no argument. You were speaking
dead-as-rock. I: flashed-marigolds.

You banged your head against the wind-flat rock
then did it again again. For you, for you

physical pain was like that newly dead glistening
Loch Ness monster we dredged up on a class trip.

for you for you, twittered the brown-beaked bird.
I should have known it was just my own chirping.

Isthmus

Your identify is my identity and vice versa.
This is the equivalent of a pineapple supreme cake.

Nietzsche, discovering the sublime one October
at an important locale, gives up searching for love.

Reading the star-filled music of the morning paper,
he relinquishes his morning raspberries.

If all he wants is power, he could be me,
screaming into crow-filled sky.

***

Morning ironing suffuses the living room
with quiet fortitude. Hot chocolate steams.

Must I reject your mistakes to be myself a mistake
as obvious as a hitchhiker's thumb transgressing the sky?

***

Months later, I find myself on a doorstep.
Wind shuffles leaves in a way that reminds me

of a child, play-sweeping the yard. In the study,
you put down your pen. I put down my pen.

We envy the shell left on the windowsill:
its quiet after the snail has gone.

Essay on What I am Most Afraid to Write About

1)

Imagine yourself, reading this poem
in bed with your monogamous lover
(your second this year?)
You count each other's compliments
like you will years later
count the compounded interest
on a missed alimony payment.

But now it is winter

and you are happy, falling asleep holding
hands, joking about the couple hospitalized
after fucking in a collapsing snowdrift.

2)

If the quality of art depends on the degree of emotion
it inflicts—as my last boyfriend argued in an unfinished essay
on why computer games should be considered art—

then the theater piece where I dress up as Socrates and administer
hemlock to the crowd of well-dressed subscribers

would be the ultimate achievement and the corpses
the rave reviews.

But art, I've heard, is supposed to
protect us from real suffering.

Pure feeling, like a body within
the sidewalk's chalk outline,
should be removed.

3)

When you close this book, I put the spacesuit on and lose
my gravity, float around my bedroom with the lights off,

the ceiling covered with glow-in-the-dark stars
arranged in false constellations.

I am the master of these stars and this dark and this quiet.

4)

Try to listen for the breakup whistle now.

At this moment, it is as far away as the call

of the bleached penguin in the California zoo my first grade teacher
described pre-nap to the horizontal class.

Did you know I pretended I could hear the penguin's song
based on her description of how it waddled?

I thought, for certain, this lie would make the teacher like me best.

5)

In college, the boy whose hair bounced throughout our senior seminar,
the one I always figured was the biggest geek, but later heard was sleeping
with the matted-hair girl who skinny-dipped in the public pool

wrote an essay on Rilke's fourth sonnet to Orpheus. He argued love
was nothing more than the realization of the un-bridgeable distance
between you and whom you loved.

I was twenty-two when I wrote my critique of his essay and at the time
so comfortable with the only real boyfriend I'd ever had that I let him pick
the dandruff off my scalp.

I was reading late William Carlos Williams and loved it when he wrote
to his wife that he thought of love not as a storm "but as a garden
that expanded." In another poem for his sixty-fifth birthday
he wrote "she kissed me while I pissed."

I thought this was a new possibility for love poetry,
freed from the anxiety of desire, and was ashamed of the years
I'd spent admiring Rilke's praise of the unrequited. I hated his silent
pregnant women with their terrifying self-indulgent beauty.
        Dumb Sappho,
I thought, blushing like burning grass. Why couldn't she love
a girl who was already hers?

Years later a friend said, "Yeah, Williams wrote his wife some nice poems,
but he was cheating on her the whole time. Everyone knew."

6)

When I am alone, I think the pencil's lead smells like a horse stable
        in Connecticut.

When I am with another, I say it smells like mud washed away by a storm.

Is one analogy more authentic than another?

No pencil smells like any other.

Mud in Connecticut is indistinguishable from a horse stable washed
        away by a storm.

7)

If loneliness is going to be a song,
let the song
be so loud that the ears of all the un-lonely
are permanently damaged.

If it's not, I could just
as well be a mime,
scaling the walls of aloneness
for an audience of pink stuffed llamas.

If loneliness is just a work of art—

some poem or some song or a play—

I don't really want it. Any of it.

It has taken me my whole life to be able to write this.

So flat it is barely a poem.

I want my language to be this flat.

Flat.

Too flat to be a fucking poem!

Dear reader, forget you thought,

you ever thought

this could have been a poem.

PRAYERS FOR BUSINESS

King's Song

Baby, give me your nothing.
Your silent ears split from each other
like halves of a cracked

piggy bank. Baby, lucky,
lucky to be a baby. Can't I—why—
can't I—why—rattle

about in your ugly ugh
ugh ocean. Me, another made
king made. I have to smile

on every coin's back,
have to give an image
of myself away

each day, exchange
my face for one worth less
or "less." Baby,

make me *your*
nothing. My daylight
is already wide.

Five springtimes—
minus one—
die. Die?

Each baby's almost
babied and babying—
almost, but never,

never yet, not.

Five Prayers for Business

The stillness of an orange hamburger drive-in.
What we call "the living" are not its neon progeny.

Release us, oh mighty, from this mighty hotdog.
Release me, oh hotdog, from this mighty language.

***

She strips off her organs and swims fully clothed
under the trademarked moon.

A hired crooner snores next to a throatless frog.
A featherless bird devours the remains of a fried chicken.

Mother, where is the blood that was dripping
through the earlobe of the doll I sucked at three?

***

Silence. Some victory?

When Dionysius dipped into his silk dress
and earrings, no paper-pusher whispered:

"The private is sacred."

This would be the end of accounting.

***

Despite our waltz through the sleeping briefcase,
despite the brass bowl or the white apple,

all wires promise the idea of future wires.

***

O.K. So you found the insignificance of business
disappointing. You worry that we're just words

projected on the living: two mice in a cavern,
casting elongated shadows on an idea.

Would you rather be dead? Would you rather
dye your hair the color of cinders?

Jeez.

How Jejune Is This Apocalypse, Hon?

Freed from his fourth relational verticality seminar,
our favorite eidetic sax player serenades

Babylonian Barbie, model eight, as she burns
the future devil's nose hair for their pre-ironic date.

You get the driftwood.

Crimes of art indistinguishable
from crimes of religion.

Lots of hyphens and neutered rats are all
anyone needs to hide emotional loss.

The swirling Wall Street circus
swallowed by the sea's missing shore

is just another emblem for the orgasmic
inner burning of a modest star.

Spools in the airport's slot
machine painted solid black.

A separate Mona Lisa smiles on
every side of the Louvre brand Rubik's cube.

They say all you need to do is twist it
and you will find your own face.

Color by Numbers (The Landscape Set)

Rural Scene

The deer droppings are here and the rooster's
memory of its birth is here too.

They glisten, pink, as if described
in a dumb kid's science report or a poem.

In the corner, the moon removes
its glow in the dark condom.

Cowboys make the best presidents,
the billboard declares. Not being a ghost myself,

I believe it when I hear the color orange contains
the chewed gum of only the happiest children.

Suburban Scene

Two toddlers lick powdered candy by the aqua-
painted swimming pool. I wish I was one of those

purple bikini ladies who read magazines
about difficult sex positions while their children

smash into each other in the wading pool.
Instead, I am the number three around the white

unpainted space above the head of the tall
teenager who lingers on the ladder to the high dive.

She's thinking again about how
it's possible to think about not thinking.

This blue might as well be the final arbiter of summer.
You'd have to be a virgin to care where it ends.

Pre-Apocalyptic Scene

There are tourists, complete with fanny packs
and guide books, in my own green bedroom.

Under the sheets, they glance at the brown
newspaper clippings about our twins'

marriage to and divorce from each other.
Its language is the color of our parrot

if the bird was dipped in yellow. Please understand
if I pick my nose and study it under this light,

it's only because I want to confront the texture
of the paint that created and will one day eradicate me.

City Scene

In a store window, a history of art
begins with a battle painted on a pot

and ends with a model of Duchamp's
urinal next to a couture bustier.

A man in a T-shirt for a topless bar
slips a twenty into his wife's palm.

In another store window, a book of holidays:
a witch snuggles Abe Lincoln, a robot turkey

dances the lindy with a pink Easter bunny
while our dear Ms. Claus, hair in the air

and thin from her grapefruit diet,
smothers the teal Cupid at her breast.

Diaries from a 21st Century House

1)

I take another swig of liquid nitrogen.
The rocket ship from a Cub Scout's wallpaper

circles the limits of my burgeoning ego
while the boy whose pigtail I once pulled breathes

fiercely into his new brain as it were a fresh
Cracker Jack exploding in a closed mouth.

2)

All of the old ways of being have left the empty theater. I stand on
a platform, floating above an urban dock trying to remember what
it felt like to be three and in the woods. This was the first of the
many ends of poetry. The second involved a match in a locker
room in Kansas. The third involved a red Chevrolet and a manual
written with a toothpick on my skin.

Now I write business memos for a mail-order identity firm.

An acquaintance encourages his girlfriend to inject chemicals to
prolong the life of a cookie which was never real. She says her job
is supposed to be about "packaging."

"Dear failed customer," I attempt to begin, but always a desk fan
lets loose its ornate melody; and I am stuck wearing more than my
clothes again.

3)

"If you want to rid the house of vermin, you'd be better off
writing poetry or some other such gesture of a stunted masculinity,"

I say to the short man telling tall tales at a dwindling party.
Does this mean the insects crawling the wall are just

another manifestation of an opulent mind, that good
Protestants only use the word "Baroque" out of fear?

I had been waiting to tell him that "with you,
I could become female in spring," but by then,

something had already blown my hairy breath back,
curled it, like the kite-like question mark of my dick...

How lovely we could both have been—
cat-walking through the airport

in matching stolen swollen swimsuits,
dark flames from the soda pop factory burning our insides out!

May 26, 2000

Pigeons arrive at my window in leg braces.

The honey in our national defense
sticking to the data, quote unquote.

Someone needs to quarantine these results.

"Music is only politics if you're
tone deaf or have a conscience."

Neither of which is a problem if the air conditioner

in the inherited Buick drones over
the Rachel Carson tape. What sings

is quantifiable as the fingerprint of an actual dead
woman found in a linguistic toaster oven.

(At least the appliance received health care!)

Still, when the frigid quarters in our pockets
contemplate the new white plates

at the disco bowling alley of aquatic mistakes

it's as if every six years we were given a kazoo
so powerful it could blow brains into and out of position's

billowing wig.

From "The Diaries of the Manner Turned"

She

The frescos of our illegitimate president, still wet,
glisten like plantation stars, shiny in the antebellum
darkness of a make-believe youth. We try to dodge this
hospitality, preferring the equine lull of a crystalline pale.
Me, feminine in earmuffs and a sparkling new nose. You,
wolverine and cruel, mouthing "The Star Spangled Banana"
in striped boxers and fake code.

He

The skeleton raincoat is inside out.
I'm almost naked at the drive-through car wash,
my new wife's anger another male peacock
without mirror, strutting around our pink-
themed fort. "We had wanted an equilibrium
of means, if not of ends" droned the manicured-
lawn gnome, the dream-life doublespeak
spooling over and out, squeaking beyond.

It

The rising cost of Ferris wheel parts hindered
the ability to fly. This was tough on Dad. Another
action figure's dream life deferred. What's a family
without a gun to heave and scold? We wake up
nature and it spits us out. Alert as an erect back
splinter in the brain, immune to rubber gloves.
Dark ruins of apologetic trees dissolve the hemispheres
like skin. Without a flesh. Shield.

Return to Normalcy

9/25 — 10/03, 2001

1)

Companies advertise their brands
with statements of sympathy.

Every multinational corporation
adds a U.S. flag to their sign

while our President grits his teeth to cover
the sound of malfunctioning palm pilots.

2)

It's thundering at 1am which reminds me of the sound of the crash
which I thought was thunder. I'm shaking and alone—half sleeping
at the door of a nightmare. There I convince the dream terrorists
that if they let me walk back home in the bottomless shopping cart
they use for hauling people to their death, I'll tell everyone who
passes I'm already dead. They acquiesce to my request and I think
to myself that I'm like one of the Jewish guards, guiding the other
Jews, whom I don't know at all, to their death. When a thin woman
approaches I say to her, "I'm a metal railing. I'll help to keep you
in."

3)

On Fulton, a man in purple
is giddy with apocalyptic hope.

"White devils. Jews." Blah blah blah.
I ask "Can't you see how hating

people causes death?" He says
"No men flew those planes.

That was God. God loves to hate."

4)

In the Sung period, when Su Tung-p'o asks "what is the Northern Dipper or the Southern Sieve but a household utensil?" This is centuries after a previous final blow to irony. Still, like the woman with the sharpened fingernails who can't pick up the tomato she wants to cook, irony remains in the same aisle because it still hasn't completed its job. It takes a long time to fold the map of tragedy into a paper hat. Blood keeps getting in the way of the crease. Already, the Speaker is holding a press conference to change the name of the war. Already, the ads for the new fall programming are in. Soon it will start raining again on the children whom our army doesn't even need to kill in order to let die.

How Many More Minutes Until We Can Devour Our Breached Contract?

Florida

A pink gondola floats
into a false
memory (1953).
The gingham
dress of an ideal
mother flutters
like a sky-sized
eyelash

while the state's
original pill jar,
now empty,
rolls down
the mall's
sealed hall.

Texas

Balls bounce against prison walls, calling out *now, now, now*
with each hard hit.
The red cooked body of a wannabe swimsuit model models
new pink guns
to soccer moms
in bee-decorated tees.

YES! The whole state a parking lot, a raccoon utopia,
a sport utility vehicle made of PURE LOVE,

a nuclear-powered banana split,
split open

so we can lick
its inner cold.

Town and Country, Missouri

A dream of golf course infinity:

weed whackers at war with sit-down tractors
trimming the park for high-on-coffee
highway commuters
to glance at on their drive to work.

Please don't desecrate our symbol
by washing your hands
with the U.S. flag soap,

a father thinks, but doesn't say
in his über-dad wing chair.
Silent, he watches his *Time-Life* videos
of the last good war.

Seattle

The corner
where we kissed
in the rain,
where my books
heavy with logic
and long overdue
made me hunch
in his shadow
with joy
is now
the corner
the reporters
stand on
for the ten
o'clock news,
while my
neighbors,
whom I never
knew,
rush

inside,
wash
the tear
gas
from
their eyes.

Connecticut

Henry Ford, in Michigan, builds his home
far from the road to hide the sounds
of the road, while Wallace Stevens hits
one golf ball into two Memphis Jars.

Look, these lines are on white.
White, like the skin that's supposed
to protect me from the burden
of history or the guns of the police

or like that idea of twenty Connecticuts,
marching over and through twenty other
identical yet unknowable Connecticuts,
sleeping in some patrician dark.

Washington, D.C.

Deemed the hot couple by *E Weekly!*
John and Abigail continue writing letters

to each other from the grave. The recycled water
in their memorial fountain smells like the pool

where a teenage boy (circa 1974) grabs a girl's
padded breast until she cries.

How many more Abe Lincolns will it take to sell
the designer corkscrew to the Japanese?

Cincinnati is burning again
the way our capital rarely burns:

The real city, and our idea of it,
both burning, as if they were

connected
like a man's two hands.

4 2/09